Alberta D. Jones

FATAL FURY CITY
OF THE WOLVES
GAME GUIDE

Essential Tips, Combos, and Strategies for Victory

Chapter 1: Introduction to City of the Wolves........................5

  1.1 Overview of the Fatal Fury Series........................5

  1.2 What's New in City of the Wolves 7

  1.3 Game Platforms & Release Info 10

  1.4 How This Guide Is Structured 13

Chapter 2: Game Modes Breakdown........................17

  2.1 Story Mode 17

  2.2 Arcade Mode 20

  2.3 Versus & Online Multiplayer 24

  2.4 Training & Tutorials........................29

Chapter 3: Core Mechanics & Controls 35

  3.1 Arcade vs Smart Style Controls........................35

  3.2 Basic Movement & Inputs........................37

  3.3 Combos, Cancels & Chain Techniques........................39

  3.4 Understanding the Rev System 41

Chapter 4: Defensive Play & Counters........................43

  4.1 Blocking & Perfect Guard........................43

  4.2 Dodging, Rolls & Recovery 44

  4.3 Breaks, Parries, and Counter-Attacks........................46

  4.4 Defensive Use of the Rev System........................48

Chapter 5: Character Roster Overview 49

  5.1 Returning Fighters (Terry, Mai, Joe, Andy, etc.)........................49

  5.2 New Faces (Vox Reaper, etc.)........................52

  5.3 Guest Fighters (Cristiano Ronaldo, Salvatore Ganacci)
........................53

  5.4 Character Archetypes & Fighting Styles........................55

Chapter 6: In-Depth Character Guides 57

    6.1 Move Lists & Input Commands 57

    6.2 Strategy & Best Matchups 59

    6.3 Combos & Rev Techniques 61

    6.4 Style Customization & Loadouts 64

Chapter 7: Stages, Arenas & Environmental Factors 67

    7.1 Stage List & Descriptions 67

    7.2 Interactive Elements & Hazards 70

    7.3 Dynamic Stage Transitions 72

    7.4 Stage Selection Strategy 74

Chapter 8: Multiplayer & Online Strategy 76

    8.1 Ranked vs Casual Play 76

    8.2 Building a Competitive Loadout 77

    8.3 Lag & Netcode Optimization Tips 79

    8.4 Reading Your Opponent 81

Chapter 9: Unlockables, Easter Eggs & Secrets 83

    9.1 Hidden Characters & Costumes 83

    9.2 Unlockable Stages & Themes 84

    9.3 Easter Eggs & Series References 86

    9.4 Tips for 100% Completion 87

Chapter 10: Advanced Techniques & Meta Play 90

    10.1 Frame Data & Hitbox Mastery 90

    10.2 Mix-ups, Pressure, and Punishes 92

    10.3 Tournament Play Essentials 94

    10.4 Post-Launch Updates & DLC Strategy 95

Chapter 1: Introduction to City of the Wolves

1.1 Overview of the Fatal Fury Series

The *Fatal Fury* series, known in Japan as *Garou Densetsu* (Legend of the Hungry Wolf), is one of SNK's most iconic and influential fighting game franchises. It first debuted in 1991 with *Fatal Fury: King of Fighters* on the Neo Geo arcade and home systems, and quickly became a staple of the 1990s fighting game boom, standing proudly alongside heavyweights like *Street Fighter* and *Mortal Kombat*.

The Origins

Fatal Fury was designed by Takashi Nishiyama, one of the original creators of *Street Fighter*. This lineage is evident in the game's core mechanics, which emphasize one-on-one martial arts combat, precise inputs, and special move execution. Unlike many other fighters of the time, *Fatal Fury* placed strong emphasis on storytelling, with a central narrative revolving around two brothers—**Terry and Andy Bogard**—seeking revenge against the crime boss **Geese Howard**, who murdered their adoptive father, Jeff Bogard.

Innovation in Fighting Games

What made *Fatal Fury* stand out was its innovative **two-lane battle system**, allowing players to hop between foreground and background planes during combat. This mechanic added a strategic layer to matches and separated the series from other 2D fighters.

Later entries, such as *Fatal Fury 3* and *Real Bout Fatal Fury*, introduced even more lanes, destructible environments, and more fluid combo systems.

Over time, SNK refined and expanded the series, introducing new characters, deeper story arcs, and more complex gameplay systems. The franchise eventually culminated in the release of *Garou: Mark of the Wolves* in 1999—a major reboot that featured a time skip, a fresh new cast, and a more grounded, technical fighting system. It remains a beloved classic, praised for its tight mechanics, mature art style, and deep competitive potential.

Legacy and Influence

The *Fatal Fury* series laid the groundwork for other SNK properties, most notably *The King of Fighters* series, which began as a crossover of characters from *Fatal Fury*, *Art of Fighting*, and other SNK titles. Characters like **Terry Bogard**, **Mai Shiranui**, and **Geese Howard** have since become icons in the fighting game world, often appearing in other games like *Super Smash Bros. Ultimate*, *Capcom vs. SNK*, and *Tekken 7*.

Even during the years without new mainline entries, the series maintained a loyal fanbase, with *Garou: Mark of the Wolves* enjoying a cult following and frequent tournament play. It was re-released on numerous modern platforms and is still considered one of the finest 2D fighters ever made.

The Road to City of the Wolves

After more than two decades, SNK officially announced *Fatal Fury: City of the Wolves* in 2022, reigniting interest in the franchise. The game is a direct successor to *Garou*, continuing the storylines of characters like **Rock Howard** and introducing new faces and modern mechanics, while preserving the franchise's roots in gritty, street-level martial arts action.

City of the Wolves represents both a revival and an evolution— designed to appeal to longtime fans of the series while welcoming a new generation of players to SNK's legacy of intense, stylish fighting games.

1.2 What's New in City of the Wolves

After over two decades of silence, SNK has returned to the *Fatal Fury* series with *City of the Wolves*, and it's not just a nostalgic throwback—it's a modern reimagining built for today's fighting game scene. While it honors its roots, *City of the Wolves* introduces a suite of new features, systems, and design philosophies that refresh the gameplay while staying true to the soul of the series. Here's what makes this entry stand out:

A New Visual Identity

One of the first things players will notice is the game's **bold cel-shaded art style**. Inspired by anime and classic 2D sprite aesthetics, the visuals are clean, vibrant, and full of personality. The animation is fluid and expressive, capturing each character's fighting spirit while making every punch, kick, and super move visually satisfying.

This visual overhaul modernizes the game while paying homage to SNK's rich 2D legacy. From the neon-lit streets to the atmospheric backdrops, *City of the Wolves* delivers a stylized but gritty world that fits the tone of the series perfectly.

The Rev System – Power, Flow, and Flexibility

The biggest gameplay innovation comes with the introduction of the **Rev System**. This core mechanic adds a dynamic layer to combat and offers players new ways to express their style:

- **Rev Arts**: Enhanced versions of special moves that consume a Rev Gauge, similar to EX moves in other fighters.

- **Rev Blow**: A cinematic, high-impact attack that can turn the tide of a match if timed correctly.

- **Rev Guard**: A powerful defensive mechanic that lets you block attacks with reduced knockback and chip damage.

- **Rev Accel**: A combo extender mechanic that lets players link special moves for flashy and effective combos.

The Rev System emphasizes **versatility**, allowing both offensive and defensive players to utilize it in different ways. It encourages experimentation and adapts to multiple playstyles, making it accessible for newcomers and deep enough for veterans.

Dual Control Schemes – Arcade Style vs. Smart Style

City of the Wolves introduces **two control schemes**:

- **Arcade Style**: Classic SNK inputs for players who prefer precision, quarter-circle motions, and full manual control.

- **Smart Style**: A simplified input mode, allowing for easier execution of special moves and combos with single-button commands or shortcuts.

This dual setup ensures that the game is welcoming to beginners while still retaining the technical depth that hardcore players love. It's a significant step toward making the game more inclusive without sacrificing competitiveness.

A Mix of Old and New Fighters

The roster in *City of the Wolves* blends **returning legends, next-gen warriors**, and even **guest characters**:

- Veterans like **Terry Bogard, Mai Shiranui, Andy Bogard,** and **Joe Higashi** return, with updated movesets and visuals.

- Newcomers like **Vox Reaper** bring fresh energy and unique fighting styles to the table.

- Guest appearances from **Cristiano Ronaldo** and **DJ Salvatore Ganacci** add a wildcard element that's both surprising and controversial, drawing interest from beyond the traditional fighting game community.

Each character has been carefully designed to feel distinct, both in playstyle and personality, offering a diverse lineup that caters to different types of players.

Expanded Story & Lore

While past *Fatal Fury* games hinted at lore through pre-fight dialogues and arcade endings, *City of the Wolves* expands on storytelling with a more structured narrative, character-specific cutscenes, and a deeper dive into the world post-*Garou: Mark of the Wolves*. Expect returning rivalries, evolving character arcs, and mysterious new threads that tie back to the past while paving the way for future installments.

1.3 Game Platforms & Release Info

Fatal Fury: City of the Wolves is set to launch on **April 24, 2025**, bringing the classic fighting franchise into the modern era. The game will be available on a variety of platforms, ensuring that fans across different systems can jump into the action. Below are the platforms and additional release information for the game:

Supported Platforms

Fatal Fury: City of the Wolves will be available on the following platforms:

- **PlayStation 5 (PS5)**

- **PlayStation 4 (PS4)**

- **Xbox Series X|S**

- **PC (Steam & Epic Games Store)**

These platforms ensure broad accessibility, whether you're playing on the latest consoles or enjoying the game on a powerful gaming PC. The game will feature cross-platform play, allowing you to battle friends no matter what system they're using.

Pre-order Bonuses & Early Access

For those eager to dive into the game early, pre-ordering *Fatal Fury: City of the Wolves* offers several bonuses:

- **Early Access**: Players who pre-order will gain access to the game **three days earlier**, starting from **April 21, 2025**. This gives fans a head start to explore the new mechanics and characters before the official release date.

- **Exclusive Costume**: Pre-ordering will also unlock a special DLC **Terry Bogard Costume** inspired by his classic look in *Fatal Fury 2*. This adds a nostalgic touch for long-time fans of the series.

Special Editions & Pricing

Fatal Fury: City of the Wolves will be available in a **Standard Edition** and **Special Edition**:

- **Standard Edition**: Includes the base game for the platform of your choice.

- **Special Edition**: Priced at **$59.99 / €59.99**, this edition includes the base game as well as the **Season Pass** for additional downloadable content (DLC) in the future, which may include extra characters, costumes, and stages.

The Special Edition is perfect for players who want to fully experience the game's post-launch content as soon as it becomes available.

System Requirements for PC

For players on PC, here are the **minimum system requirements** to run the game smoothly:

- **OS**: Windows 10

- **Processor**: Intel Core i5-7500 / AMD Ryzen 3 1200

- **Memory**: 8 GB RAM

- **Graphics**: GTX 1060 (6GB VRAM) / Radeon RX 580 (4GB VRAM)

- **DirectX**: Version 12

- **Storage**: 60 GB of available space

These requirements ensure that *City of the Wolves* runs smoothly on most modern gaming PCs. For optimal performance, a higher-end system will provide a smoother experience, especially with higher frame rates and resolutions.

Global Release Information

The game will launch simultaneously across all regions on **April 24, 2025**. Fans in North America, Europe, Japan, and other regions can expect to play the game on the same day. Pre-order bonuses and special editions may vary slightly depending on the region, so be sure to check the official website or digital storefronts for details on what's available in your area.

1.4 How This Guide Is Structured

This game guide is designed to provide both newcomers and seasoned *Fatal Fury* veterans with the tools, strategies, and knowledge necessary to master *City of the Wolves*. The guide is organized in a way that ensures you can easily navigate through the different aspects of the game, whether you're looking for basic gameplay explanations or advanced tactics.

Chapter Breakdown

The guide is divided into **10 main chapters**, each focusing on a different aspect of the game. Each chapter contains multiple sections, which are clearly marked for easy reference. Here's how each chapter is organized:

- **Chapter 1: Introduction to City of the Wolves**
  This chapter provides a broad overview of the *Fatal Fury* series, the new features in *City of the Wolves*, and essential information about the game's release and platform options. It's meant to give players a clear understanding of what to expect from the game and how it fits into the long history of the franchise.

- **Chapter 2: Game Modes Breakdown**
  In this chapter, we delve into the different game modes offered in *City of the Wolves*, from Story Mode to Online Multiplayer. Each mode is explained in detail, with tips on how to approach them, whether you're aiming for a single-player experience or competitive online play.

- **Chapter 3: Core Mechanics & Controls**
  This chapter explains the fundamentals of the game, including the new control schemes, special moves, and how

the Rev System functions. We cover everything from basic movement to advanced mechanics, ensuring you understand the flow of combat.

- **Chapter 4: Defensive Play & Counters**
  City of the Wolves is not just about attacking—it's also about defense. In this chapter, we break down techniques like blocking, dodging, and counter-attacking. We explain how to use defensive mechanics effectively to turn the tide of battle in your favor.

- **Chapter 5: Character Roster Overview**
  Here, we explore the game's diverse roster of characters, including both returning fighters and newcomers. Each character's fighting style, strengths, and weaknesses are discussed to help you choose your preferred fighter.

- **Chapter 6: In-Depth Character Guides**
  If you want to dive deeper into specific characters, this chapter is for you. Each fighter's move list, strategies, and combos are outlined in detail. We also include tips on how to best utilize each character's strengths in different matchups.

- **Chapter 7: Stages, Arenas & Environmental Factors**
  Every stage in *City of the Wolves* has its own unique features. This chapter covers the different arenas, interactive elements, and hazards that can impact a fight, helping you understand how to use the environment to your advantage.

- **Chapter 8: Multiplayer & Online Strategy**
  For those looking to compete against others, this chapter focuses on multiplayer and online play. We provide advice on how to build a competitive loadout, optimize your online

experience, and read your opponent's strategies.

- **Chapter 9: Unlockables, Easter Eggs & Secrets**
  City of the Wolves is packed with hidden content. In this chapter, we uncover the unlockable characters, costumes, stages, and Easter eggs that will reward curious players and completionists.

- **Chapter 10: Advanced Techniques & Meta Play**
  The final chapter is aimed at experienced players looking to master advanced gameplay techniques. We discuss frame data, hitbox mastery, mix-ups, and pressure tactics, as well as tips for competitive play in tournaments.

Sub-Chapters and Sections

Each chapter is broken down into **sub-chapters** and individual **sections** to make finding information easy. Whether you're looking for detailed character guides or general gameplay strategies, the structure of the guide ensures that you can quickly jump to the section you need.

- **Easy Navigation**: Each chapter and section is clearly numbered, making it simple to reference specific topics.

- **Step-by-Step Guides**: Some sections, like combo execution or character strategies, are presented in step-by-step formats, allowing you to follow along and master the moves.

- **Visual Aids**: Where applicable, images and illustrations are included to highlight key points, like combos or move inputs. These visual aids help break down complex concepts and make them easier to grasp.

Additional Features

- **Tips and Tricks**: Throughout the guide, we include helpful tips and hidden strategies that can give you an edge in your matches.

- **Glossary**: For new players, a glossary of terms (such as "frame data," "linking combos," etc.) is provided at the end of the guide to ensure that everyone can follow along.

- **Updates and DLC**: Post-launch updates and downloadable content (DLC) will be covered in the last section of Chapter 10, so you're always up to date with the latest changes and additions to the game.

Chapter 2: Game Modes Breakdown

2.1 Story Mode

The **Story Mode** of *Fatal Fury: City of the Wolves* is the cornerstone of the game's single-player experience. It not only introduces players to the new mechanics and characters but also continues the rich, character-driven narrative that fans of the *Fatal Fury* series have come to love. The mode is designed to be immersive, with branching storylines, emotional character arcs, and high-stakes battles that unfold through beautifully animated cutscenes.

A New Chapter in the Story

The story picks up several years after the events of *Garou: Mark of the Wolves*, where **Rock Howard** has grown into a young man, still grappling with the legacy of his father's violent past and the shadow of **Geese Howard**. In *City of the Wolves*, Rock is now caught in a new conflict that involves old rivals, new enemies, and powerful forces attempting to reshape the fighting world.

The plot centers around **the resurgence of a dangerous underground fighting organization**, aiming to overthrow the existing balance of power in the global fighting circuit. Players will find themselves taking on the roles of various fighters, each with their own personal motivations, to uncover the truth behind this shadowy organization and stop them before it's too late.

Character-Centric Storylines

The Story Mode in *City of the Wolves* is more than just a series of battles—it's a personal journey for each character. Each fighter has their own **unique storyline**, which explores their motives, relationships with other characters, and their role in the larger conflict. Some characters, like **Terry Bogard**, are motivated by a desire to protect their loved ones, while others, like **Mai Shiranui**, seek to prove themselves as warriors in the ever-evolving world of martial arts.

- **Rock Howard**'s story is central to the narrative, and players who choose him will experience the most in-depth exploration of the storyline. His journey revolves around dealing with his own inner conflict, reconciling his father's past actions, and standing against a powerful new threat.

- **Terry Bogard** is called upon to guide and mentor the younger generation of fighters, while also facing his own demons as his past and legacy as the "Legendary Hungry Wolf" are revisited.

Each character's storyline is carefully woven into the larger narrative, offering players insights into how their fighter fits into the overarching conflict.

Dynamic Dialogue & Choices

One of the standout features of the Story Mode is the **dynamic dialogue system**. As players progress through the chapters, they'll have opportunities to make **story-altering decisions** during key moments. These choices affect how characters interact with each other, leading to different paths, endings, and unlockables. This element gives the Story Mode a **replayable nature**, as players can explore multiple outcomes by choosing different options during pivotal scenes.

Additionally, players can choose the difficulty of the story's encounters, ranging from easy for casual players to challenging for competitive veterans. The higher the difficulty, the more intense the AI becomes, and more unique rewards or story branches may be unlocked.

Fights with Purpose

Each battle in the Story Mode is **thematically tied to the narrative**, making each encounter feel significant. You're not just fighting to win—you're fighting to advance the plot. Whether it's battling an old rival, protecting a loved one, or confronting a sinister new enemy, each fight serves as a key turning point in the overall narrative.

The game's **cinematic cutscenes** are used effectively to provide context before and after each major fight, giving players a deeper understanding of the stakes involved. These cutscenes feature beautifully animated sequences that delve into the characters' personal struggles and triumphs, giving the game a more cinematic, storytelling-focused feel than past entries.

Unlockables and Endings

Completing Story Mode unlocks a wide variety of rewards, including **alternate costumes**, **new playable characters**, and **bonus stages**. These unlockables provide an incentive to replay the mode and experience the story from different character perspectives.

- **Multiple Endings**: Depending on the choices made and the characters selected, Story Mode features multiple endings. Some endings are bittersweet, others triumphant, and some even hint at the future of the *Fatal Fury* series.

- **Secret Characters**: As you progress, secret characters are unlocked, adding to the game's roster. These fighters may have their own unique storylines or alternate endings that provide further lore and backstory.

Key Features

- **Cinematic Storytelling**: Beautiful, high-quality cutscenes that progress the story and deepen character development.

- **Character-Driven Narratives**: Unique storylines for each fighter, with character-specific motivations, struggles, and resolutions.

- **Choices Matter**: Key decisions that affect story outcomes and character interactions, leading to multiple playthroughs and different endings.

- **Rewarding Progression**: Unlockable content that encourages replayability, including new characters, costumes, and story routes.

2.2 Arcade Mode

Arcade Mode in *Fatal Fury: City of the Wolves* is a nostalgic throwback to the roots of the *Fatal Fury* series, offering players a traditional, single-player experience where they battle through a series of increasingly difficult opponents in a quest to reach the final boss. This mode is designed to capture the feel of classic arcade fighters, combining straightforward gameplay with the thrill of high stakes competition.

Classic Arcade Experience

In *Arcade Mode*, players take on the role of one of the game's fighters and face off against a series of CPU-controlled opponents, each with their own fighting style and difficulty level. The mode progresses through several **stages**, with each opponent becoming progressively tougher as you get closer to the final boss.

The goal is simple: defeat each opponent and challenge the **final boss** in an epic showdown. The arcade mode retains the feeling of a traditional arcade game, where you must beat a set number of enemies in a row, with the occasional mini-boss or rival character mixed in to shake things up.

Progression & Path Variations

One of the key features of *Arcade Mode* in *City of the Wolves* is the **path system**. Depending on the character you choose, the arcade path may change slightly, offering a **unique progression** through different fighters and rival encounters. This helps keep the mode fresh by ensuring that each playthrough offers a slightly different experience.

- **Standard Path**: In the most common path, you will face a traditional set of enemies leading up to the final confrontation with the game's ultimate antagonist.

- **Rival Encounters**: Some characters have specific rival fighters that they will encounter in their arcade journey.

These rivals are often tough fights that can lead to unique cutscenes and provide extra lore for that character.

- **Bonus Rounds**: As you progress, you may also encounter bonus rounds, where you face off against specific challenges (like defeating waves of enemies or executing a specific move under time pressure). These bonus rounds provide extra rewards, such as **bonus points**, **extra lives**, or **unlockable content**.

Difficulty Levels

To cater to players of all skill levels, *Arcade Mode* offers multiple difficulty settings:

- **Easy**: Perfect for new players or those just looking to experience the game's story and gameplay mechanics without the pressure of tough fights.

- **Normal**: The standard experience, offering a fair balance of challenge for most players.

- **Hard**: For experienced players who want to test their skills against the game's toughest AI opponents. Expect faster reactions, smarter tactics, and harder-hitting moves.

- **Extreme**: A hardcore difficulty setting reserved for only the most skilled players. The AI is aggressive and relentless, offering a true test of your fighting prowess.

Endings & Rewards

Just like the classic arcade fighting games, completing **Arcade Mode** grants you an ending based on the character you played as. Each fighter has their own unique ending sequence, which may include humorous, dramatic, or emotional moments that shed light on their personal journey and motivations.

Additionally, players can unlock:

- **Bonus Characters**: Completing the mode on higher difficulties or achieving certain conditions may unlock secret characters for use in other game modes.

- **Unlockable Costumes**: Some fighters have alternate outfits that can only be unlocked by completing the arcade path with specific characters or on certain difficulties.

- **Concept Art & Music**: For players interested in the behind-the-scenes aspects of the game, completing *Arcade Mode* unlocks additional concept art, soundtracks, and other collectibles that add depth to the game's world.

Replayability

Arcade Mode is built with **replayability** in mind. With multiple difficulty levels, different path variations, and unique endings for each character, there is always a reason to come back and play again. Additionally, the **high score system** encourages players to strive for the best performance possible, competing with friends or other players for the highest scores.

Key Features

- **Traditional Arcade Experience**: Battle through a series of opponents and defeat the final boss to complete the mode.

- **Path Variations**: Different paths, rival encounters, and bonus rounds provide a unique experience each time you play.

- **Multiple Difficulty Settings**: Choose from Easy, Normal, Hard, and Extreme difficulties to match your skill level.

- **Unlockables & Rewards**: Earn character endings, costumes, and bonus content by completing the mode and achieving high scores.

- **Replayability**: With different character storylines, difficulty settings, and paths to explore, *Arcade Mode* offers plenty of incentive to revisit.

2.3 Versus & Online Multiplayer

Fatal Fury: City of the Wolves introduces a dynamic **Versus Mode** and robust **Online Multiplayer** system, allowing players to battle each other in both local and online settings. Whether you're facing off against a friend on the couch or testing your skills against players around the world, these modes offer thrilling competitive action and countless hours of replayability.

Versus Mode: Local Multiplayer

Versus Mode is the perfect choice for players who want to enjoy a traditional fighting game experience with friends or family in the same room. This mode allows two players to select their favorite characters and engage in one-on-one combat.

- **Classic Head-to-Head Battles**: Each player picks a character, and the fight begins. The first player to deplete their opponent's health bar wins the match. Players can customize the rules of the fight, such as the number of rounds, time limits, and more.

- **Multiplayer Customization**: You can adjust settings like round time, stage selection, and difficulty. Players can even create custom **tournaments** with multiple rounds, or create specific matchups like a **"Rival Fight"** where two characters with a rivalry face off, adding an extra layer of narrative flair to the battle.

- **Local Play for Up to 2 Players**: Versus Mode is optimized for two-player local gameplay, perfect for couch co-op or competitive play. If you have friends over, this mode will provide hours of entertainment without the need for online connections.

Online Multiplayer: Compete Worldwide

For those who want to take their skills to the global stage, *City of the Wolves* offers a comprehensive **Online Multiplayer** mode that connects players across different platforms (cross-platform play is enabled). Online matchmaking provides a way to compete against skilled opponents worldwide, with multiple modes and features to enhance the online experience.

Ranked Matches

For players who want to test their abilities and climb the competitive ladder, **Ranked Matches** provide a highly structured experience:

- **Ranking System**: Players are assigned ranks based on their performance in ranked matches. Winning fights increases your rank, while losing causes a drop. This system ensures that you're always matched with opponents of a similar skill level, making each fight a balanced challenge.

- **Leaderboards**: Global leaderboards track the best players, creating a competitive atmosphere. Whether you're striving to make it to the top 100 or aiming for the number one spot, leaderboards provide a sense of progression and competition.

- **Seasons & Rewards**: Ranked play operates in **seasons**, with rewards given at the end of each season. The rewards range from cosmetic items, such as exclusive costumes and skins, to in-game currency used for unlocking special content. The top players of each season receive prestigious rewards and recognition within the community.

Casual Matches

If you're not focused on climbing the ranks and just want to enjoy a friendly match, **Casual Matches** are the way to go:

- **Non-Competitive Play**: Casual matches offer a laid-back, low-stakes environment where players can freely practice, experiment with new characters, or simply have fun. Wins and losses don't affect your rank, making it a great mode for honing your skills without the pressure of a ranking system.

- **Easy Access to Online Play**: Casual matches are perfect for quick and easy matchmaking. You'll be paired with opponents based on your skill level, but the stakes are much lower than in ranked play, making it ideal for beginners or those just looking to pass the time.

Team Battles & Tournaments

Online multiplayer also offers **Team Battles** and **Tournaments** for more strategic and organized play:

- **Team Battles**: In this mode, players can select a team of fighters rather than just one character. Team Battles add a layer of strategy, as you must balance the strengths and weaknesses of each fighter in your roster. Team-based combat requires coordination and strategy, as players can switch between characters during the match, making it a highly dynamic mode.

- **Tournaments**: Competitive tournaments are regularly hosted in *Fatal Fury: City of the Wolves*. These tournaments are open to all players, with large-scale events featuring knockout rounds and bracketed matches. Winners can earn exclusive prizes such as rare skins, in-game currency, and even trophy placements on the official tournament leaderboard.

Spectator Mode & Replays

For players who enjoy watching high-level play or want to learn from others, *City of the Wolves* includes a **Spectator Mode**:

- **Watch Live Matches**: Spectator Mode allows you to watch live matches between players. Whether it's a casual fight or a heated tournament match, you can spectate without directly participating in the action.

- **Replays**: You can view replays of past matches, including your own. This is a great way to study your mistakes, learn from your victories, or simply revisit exciting moments. Replays can be saved and shared with others, making it easy to showcase your skills or dissect strategies.

Matchmaking & Online Features

To ensure fair and enjoyable matches, the online multiplayer system is equipped with robust matchmaking features:

- **Smart Matchmaking System**: The matchmaking system takes into account factors such as your skill level, character preferences, and latency to ensure you're paired with opponents who offer a fair and competitive experience.

- **Connection Stability**: Online play is optimized to minimize lag and ensure smooth gameplay. With dedicated servers, the game strives to offer a stable connection for players, no matter where they are located.

- **Cross-Platform Play**: Whether you're playing on PlayStation, Xbox, or PC, the cross-platform feature ensures you can challenge any player, expanding the pool of potential opponents and increasing the overall online community's size and diversity.

Key Features

- **Local Versus Mode**: Play head-to-head with a friend locally, with customizable settings for rounds, difficulty, and special challenges.

- **Ranked Matches**: Climb the competitive ladder, earn ranks, and compete for top positions in global leaderboards.

- **Casual Matches**: Play casually without worrying about your ranking, ideal for testing new characters or just having fun.

- **Team Battles & Tournaments**: Engage in team-based fights or enter tournaments for high-stakes, competitive action.

- **Spectator Mode & Replays**: Watch high-level matches and review your past performances to improve.

- **Cross-Platform Play**: Battle players across different platforms, increasing matchmaking variety.

2.4 Training & Tutorials

Fatal Fury: City of the Wolves offers an extensive **Training Mode** and comprehensive **Tutorials** to help players of all skill levels improve their gameplay. Whether you're a newcomer to fighting games or a veteran looking to hone advanced techniques, these modes provide the perfect environment for practicing and mastering the game's mechanics.

Training Mode: Perfect Your Skills

The **Training Mode** in *City of the Wolves* is a versatile and robust system designed to allow players to practice without the pressure of an opponent. It provides a controlled environment where you can experiment with different moves, combos, and strategies to perfect your fighting skills.

Key Features of Training Mode

- **Freeform Training**: In Training Mode, players are free to experiment with any character and any move at their own pace. You can test out different combos, practice move inputs, and explore each fighter's full move list without time constraints or interruptions. This makes it an ideal place to get comfortable with new characters or refine your fighting style.

- **AI Opponent (Customizable)**: The game features a customizable AI opponent that allows you to adjust the behavior of the enemy. You can set the AI's difficulty, aggressiveness, and defense levels. This helps you simulate specific match situations, whether you're practicing offense, defense, or combo execution.

- **Combo Trials**: A built-in feature for practicing and recording combos. Players can view on-screen inputs for complex combo strings, helping them learn the precise timing and sequences needed to pull off advanced moves. This is crucial for mastering the more intricate aspects of each character's arsenal.

- **Hitbox Visualization**: *City of the Wolves* includes a feature that shows **hitboxes** and **hurtboxes** on-screen. This allows players to see the range of each attack and understand the areas in which they will connect with the opponent. It's an invaluable tool for understanding character range, timing, and spacing.

- **Frame Data**: For advanced players, Training Mode includes **frame data**, which displays the startup, active, and recovery frames for each move. This helps you understand the nuances of each character's attacks, allowing you to master things like **frame traps, punishing unsafe moves**, and **combining attacks for optimal pressure**.

- **Recording & Playback**: One of the standout features of Training Mode is the ability to **record** a sequence of moves performed by the AI and then replay it as if you were facing an actual opponent. This lets you practice reacting to specific attacks, performing counters, or testing out strategies against predictable moves.

- **Training with Friends**: If you want to practice with another player, the game allows for **local multiplayer** in Training Mode. Both players can experiment together, allowing you to practice team combos, testing strategies, or simply sharing tips in real-time.

Tutorial Mode: Learn the Basics and Advanced Tactics

The **Tutorial Mode** is designed to guide newcomers through the fundamentals of the game and gradually introduce more complex concepts. It's a perfect starting point for players who are new to the *Fatal Fury* series or fighting games in general.

Structured Lessons

The Tutorial Mode offers a **step-by-step guide** for learning the basic and advanced mechanics of *City of the Wolves*. Players can work through various levels of difficulty, each focusing on specific skills and techniques required to become proficient in the game.

- **Basic Controls**: The first lessons cover basic controls, such as movement, blocking, jumping, and using special attacks. These tutorials teach you the fundamental skills you'll need to play the game effectively.

- **Special Moves and Combos**: Once you're comfortable with the basics, the tutorial delves into special moves, basic combos, and how to link attacks together. Each tutorial level will walk you through common combos for different characters, as well as techniques like **cancelling** and **linking moves**.

- **Advanced Mechanics**: As you progress, the tutorials introduce more complex strategies, such as **counterattacking**, **frame data analysis**, and **mind games**. You'll learn how to create pressure on your opponent, when to use specific defensive moves, and how to read and react to your opponent's actions.

- **Character-Specific Lessons**: Each character in *City of the Wolves* has their own specialized tutorial lessons. These focus on their unique movesets and fighting styles. For example, if you're playing as **Rock Howard**, the tutorial will guide you through his **Wolf Gauge** system and how to use his **special abilities** to your advantage in battle.

Interactive & Hands-On

What sets the Tutorial Mode apart is its interactive approach. Each lesson is designed to be hands-on, meaning you will not only read about techniques but also perform them in real-time. The game will guide you through the motions, and feedback is provided to help you improve.

- **Practice Challenges**: As you progress through the tutorials, you'll encounter challenges that ask you to complete specific tasks, such as performing a certain combo or executing a special move under time constraints. Completing these challenges rewards you with in-game currency, character skins, or bonus content.

- **Progressive Difficulty**: The tutorials scale in difficulty, starting with simple tasks and moving to more complex challenges. This gradual learning curve ensures that new players are not overwhelmed and gives them time to build confidence before moving on to the more advanced techniques.

- **Instant Feedback**: After each lesson, players are given feedback on their performance. Whether you performed the move correctly or missed an input, the game will provide tips and corrections to help you improve. This immediate feedback system is ideal for mastering the game's more intricate mechanics.

Key Features of Training & Tutorials

- **Comprehensive Training Mode**: Experiment freely with combos, AI opponents, and hitbox visualizations. Adjust settings for attack speed, difficulty, and frame data to fine-tune your technique.

- **Step-by-Step Tutorials**: Learn the basics of movement, combat, and special moves before progressing to advanced techniques and character-specific lessons.

- **Hands-On Experience**: Perform real-time actions, with instant feedback to help you improve your timing, spacing, and execution.

- **Combo Trials & Recording**: Test out and perfect your combos with visual aids and AI recordings, helping you train for real in-game matches.

- **Character-Specific Lessons**: Understand each character's unique strengths and abilities through personalized lessons, including their special moves and advanced tactics.

- **Challenge Mode**: Unlock rewards by completing specific challenges and tests within the tutorial system.

Chapter 3: Core Mechanics & Controls

3.1 Arcade vs Smart Style Controls

In *Fatal Fury: City of the Wolves*, the **control scheme** plays a critical role in the gameplay experience. The game offers two distinct control styles: **Arcade Controls** and **Smart Style Controls**, catering to both veteran players and newcomers. Understanding the differences between these two systems is key to mastering the game's mechanics.

Arcade Controls: Classic Fighting Game Experience

The **Arcade Controls** option is designed to give players a traditional, no-nonsense experience similar to the original arcade version of the *Fatal Fury* series. Players will need to manually execute precise button inputs for all actions, including special moves, combos, and defensive maneuvers. This system emphasizes **precise timing**, **accuracy**, and **memorization** of move sequences.

- **Input Method**: Requires players to manually input quarter-circle motions, charge commands, and other traditional fighting game inputs. This style appeals to veteran fighting game players who are familiar with classic control schemes.

- **Advanced Techniques**: More advanced techniques, like **kara cancels** and **one-frame links**, are easier to execute in this mode, as the player has full control over each input. Players accustomed to traditional fighting games will find this method most intuitive.

- **Full Control**: Arcade Controls allow players to fully master the mechanics of each character by manually controlling every aspect of their movement, specials, and combo chains.

Smart Style Controls: Simplified Input for New Players

On the other hand, **Smart Style Controls** offer a more accessible, streamlined experience designed to make the game easier for new players to pick up while maintaining depth for more experienced users. This style simplifies the execution of special moves and combos, allowing players to perform complex actions with fewer button inputs.

- **Input Method**: Special moves and certain combos are automatically simplified. For example, a character's special move might be performed by pressing a single button rather than requiring a directional input plus a button press.

- **Auto-Cancels and Chain Combos**: Smart Style Controls help new players execute chain combos and canceling moves with minimal effort, reducing the learning curve for complex mechanics.

- **Assist Features**: The system includes built-in assistance, such as **auto-blocking** (for defense) and **auto-comboing** (to simplify chained combos). These features make it easier for players to focus on the basic flow of combat without getting caught up in executing precise inputs.

- **Moderate Depth**: While simplified, Smart Style Controls still allow players to learn and progress through the game. Experienced players can still challenge themselves with the system's complexity, but it provides a smoother experience for newcomers.

Which Control Scheme Should You Choose?

- **Arcade Controls**: Best for players who are familiar with traditional fighting games and want to experience a high level of control over their character's movements and attacks.

- **Smart Style Controls**: Ideal for beginners or those who want a more accessible entry into the game. It's also a great choice for players looking to focus on strategy and timing rather than complex inputs.

3.2 Basic Movement & Inputs

Mastering the **basic movement** and **input system** is the foundation of any fighting game, and *Fatal Fury: City of the Wolves* is no different. Understanding how to move your character effectively and how the game processes input commands is crucial to success.

Basic Movement

In *City of the Wolves*, characters have a wide range of mobility options, including walking, running, jumping, and crouching. Movement is essential for setting up attacks, avoiding incoming strikes, and positioning yourself for successful combos.

- **Walking**: Pressing left or right on the control stick will cause your character to walk in the respective direction. Walking is slower than running but allows for more precise positioning.

- **Running**: Double-tapping left or right on the control stick initiates a run. Running allows you to close the distance quickly, but it can be risky if used recklessly, as it leaves you open to counters.

- **Jumping**: Pressing the jump button causes your character to leap into the air. There are **short jumps**, **long jumps**, and **double jumps** (depending on the character). Understanding how to control your jump height and direction is essential for both offense and defense.

- **Crouching**: Holding the down direction on the control stick makes your character crouch. This is an essential movement for low attacks and blocking certain high attacks from opponents.

Basic Input Commands

All characters in *City of the Wolves* have a set of basic inputs that players need to be familiar with. These are the core building blocks for more advanced actions and combos.

- **Normal Attacks**: Pressing a button (light, medium, or heavy) will trigger a normal attack. Each character has a unique set of normals, with specific strengths, speeds, and ranges.

- **Directional Inputs**: Many attacks require specific directional inputs. For example, pressing **down + attack** will execute a low attack, while **back + attack** could trigger a defensive strike.

- **Special Moves**: Special moves require precise directional inputs followed by button presses (e.g., **quarter-circle forward + punch** for a fireball). Learning these commands is critical for offensive play.

- **Blocking**: Holding the back direction while standing or crouching will make your character block attacks. **Jumping** or **dashing forward** are also forms of evasion but require proper timing to avoid attacks.

Combining Inputs for Movement & Attacks

Many advanced moves require a combination of the above inputs in quick succession, such as using a **dash** (quick forward movement) followed by a **special move**. Successful players must develop muscle memory for these combinations to flow smoothly and consistently during matches.

3.3 Combos, Cancels & Chain Techniques

Combos, cancels, and **chain techniques** are advanced gameplay mechanics that allow players to create devastating attack sequences and maintain offensive pressure. Mastering these techniques is key to becoming proficient in *Fatal Fury: City of the Wolves*.

Combos

Combos are strings of attacks that, when performed correctly, allow the player to link multiple hits together in a single flow, preventing the opponent from blocking or countering. Combos are essential for dealing large amounts of damage.

- **Basic Combos**: These are simple combos that involve linking normal attacks in a fluid sequence. For example, light punch > heavy punch > special move.

- **Combo Timing**: The key to successful combos is **timing**. Most combos require a precise window between attacks to ensure that the opponent remains in a **stun state** long enough for you to land subsequent hits.

- **Air Combos**: Some characters have **air combos**, where you can juggle your opponent in mid-air after launching them with an attack. These are often more advanced and require good timing and positioning.

Cancels

Cancels are a technique used to interrupt an attack's animation and immediately transition into another move. This allows for extended combos and faster follow-ups.

- **Special Move Cancels**: One of the most useful cancels is the **special move cancel**, where you can interrupt a normal attack with a special move (e.g., canceling a punch into a fireball). This allows for fluid, unpredictable attacks.

- **Super Cancels**: Advanced players can cancel into **super moves** or **EX specials**, extending combos and doing massive damage.

Chain Combos

Chain Combos are attacks that are linked together without relying on strict timing. In this system, pressing multiple buttons rapidly can trigger a sequence of moves that automatically flow into one another.

- **Button Chains**: Pressing buttons in rapid succession will automatically trigger a sequence of moves, allowing players to chain multiple attacks without worrying about exact timing.

- **Character-Specific Chains**: Some characters have **unique chain techniques** that allow them to link multiple attacks together in ways other characters cannot. Mastering these chains can be essential for creating a consistent and devastating offensive strategy.

3.4 Understanding the Rev System

The **Rev System** is a unique mechanic in *Fatal Fury: City of the Wolves* that adds a layer of strategy to both offensive and defensive play. The Rev System is a gauge that builds over time, providing players with access to powerful abilities and moves when it reaches certain thresholds.

What is the Rev System?

The **Rev System** is essentially a power meter that builds up during the course of a match. It fills as you perform attacks, take damage, and engage in various in-game actions. When full, it can be used to trigger a **Rev Move**, a powerful ability that can turn the tide of battle.

- **Building the Gauge**: The Rev Gauge fills up over time as you engage in combat. It fills faster when you're attacking and using special moves but also builds when you take damage or successfully block attacks.

- **Rev Moves**: Once the gauge is full, players can activate a **Rev Move**, which typically provides an advantage, such as enhanced attacks, increased speed, or access to special abilities. Some Rev Moves are unique to specific characters and can change the flow of combat.

- **Rev Burst**: In certain situations, players can trigger a **Rev Burst**, which allows them to unleash a devastating, high-damage combo or special move. It can be a game-changing tactic when used correctly at the right moment.

Strategic Use of the Rev System

Understanding when to use your Rev gauge is a critical aspect of strategy. You can choose to hold onto it for a critical moment or use it early for a powerful advantage. Players must balance their offensive and defensive actions, as managing the Rev gauge efficiently can lead to victory in close matches.

Chapter 4: Defensive Play & Counters

4.1 Blocking & Perfect Guard

Blocking is one of the most fundamental defensive techniques in *Fatal Fury: City of the Wolves*, allowing players to mitigate damage and control the pace of the match. However, effective blocking alone may not always be enough, which is why mastering the **Perfect Guard** is crucial for advanced players.

Basic Blocking

Blocking is a core mechanic in any fighting game, and *City of the Wolves* is no different. To block, simply hold the **back** direction on your control stick (for standing blocks) or **down** (for crouching blocks). By doing so, your character will negate most incoming attacks, whether they're high, mid, or low, depending on the block position.

- **High Block**: Hold **back** to block attacks that come from above, like punches or jumps.

- **Low Block**: Hold **down** to block low-hitting attacks like sweeps or certain special moves.

Perfect Guard

The **Perfect Guard** is a higher-level defensive technique that allows players to reduce damage to zero and sometimes even retaliate immediately. It requires precise timing and knowledge of your opponent's attacks.

- **How to Perform a Perfect Guard**: To execute a Perfect Guard, you need to press back to block **just as the opponent's attack is about to connect**. Timing this perfectly results in the attack being completely negated, and in some cases, it can provide a slight opening for counter-attacks.

- **Benefits of Perfect Guard**: Perfectly blocking an attack not only negates damage but also opens up opportunities for immediate counterplay. When you successfully execute a Perfect Guard, your opponent might be left in a vulnerable state, allowing you to punish them with a combo or a quick attack.

Challenges of Perfect Guard

While the Perfect Guard is a powerful tool, it's not easy to pull off. It requires excellent reaction time and deep understanding of your opponent's move patterns. If you mistime it, you will still take the full damage from the attack, so practicing Perfect Guard timing in **Training Mode** is highly recommended.

4.2 Dodging, Rolls & Recovery

While blocking is essential, sometimes avoiding the attack entirely is the best defense. *City of the Wolves* offers several evasive options, including **dodging**, **rolling**, and **recovery** mechanics, all of which are essential for creating space, avoiding damage, and turning the tide of battle in your favor.

Dodging

Dodging is a quick and versatile defensive maneuver that allows players to avoid incoming attacks entirely. Depending on your character, dodging can be done in various ways, such as through **quick sidesteps** or **backdashes**.

- **Quick Sidestep**: A quick tap of the control stick left or right while pressing the **dodge button** (or a directional input) will make your character sidestep the opponent's attack, allowing you to reposition yourself and escape pressure.

- **Backdash**: A **backdash** is performed by quickly tapping back twice. It gives your character a slight retreating movement, providing distance between you and your opponent, which is useful for avoiding oncoming attacks while staying in the fight.

Rolls

Rolls are another evasive option, performed by pressing the **dodge button** in a specific direction (forward or backward) while being hit by certain attacks or after an attack animation.

- **Forward Roll**: A **forward roll** allows you to roll toward your opponent to close the distance, either to apply pressure or to move out of a corner.

- **Backward Roll**: The **backward roll** provides a quick retreat, helping you avoid aggressive pressure from your opponent, especially when you're cornered.

Rolls are also effective for escaping throws and recovering from knockdowns. Timing and placement are critical, as a roll can be countered by a well-timed attack.

Recovery

Recovery is an essential part of defensive play, as getting knocked down leaves you vulnerable. Players need to know how to recover quickly after being knocked down to avoid further punishment.

- **Teching (Rebounding from Knockdown)**: After being knocked down, pressing a button in the right direction allows you to **tech** or **rebound**, getting back on your feet faster. Teching effectively can help you avoid being hit with follow-up attacks after a knockdown.

- **Knockdown Recovery Options**: You have the option to recover by either rolling or getting up with a quick counter, depending on the situation. Some characters can use **unique recovery moves** to regain their stance quicker and with more counter options.

4.3 Breaks, Parries, and Counter-Attacks

Defensive play isn't just about blocking and dodging— understanding how to **break** your opponent's offense, **parry** incoming attacks, and **counter-attack** effectively is essential for high-level play.

Breaks (Guard Breaks & Throw Breaks)

Breaks are techniques that disrupt your opponent's offense and give you the opportunity to turn the tables.

- **Guard Breaks**: Some special moves and charged attacks can break through your opponent's guard, forcing them to stagger or become temporarily vulnerable. These moves are vital for breaking through the defenses of players who rely too much on blocking.

  - **How to Perform a Guard Break**: Typically, a Guard Break occurs when you land a special move or attack with a charged or heavy attribute that goes through a block. Certain characters have attacks specifically designed to break through an opponent's defense.

- **Throw Breaks**: **Throw breaks** are essential for escaping grabs and throws. When an opponent attempts a throw, you can break free by pressing the correct button at the precise moment. Throwing becomes a critical strategy to keep your opponent guessing between standard attacks and grabs.

Parries

A **parry** is a defensive technique that involves deflecting an incoming attack with precision, leaving the opponent vulnerable to a counter.

- **Performing a Parry**: To execute a parry, you need to input a defensive move (like blocking or a certain directional input) just as the opponent's attack is about to land. A successful parry will deflect the attack and often leave your opponent open for a quick counter.

- **Perfect Parries**: In certain situations, if you **time the parry perfectly,** your character may not only deflect the attack but also gain an advantage like increased damage or extra knockback.

Counter-Attacks

Counter-attacks allow you to punish an opponent's offensive mistake by hitting them with an attack at the moment they are vulnerable.

- **Punish Moves**: After successfully blocking or parrying an attack, you can **immediately perform a counter** to punish your opponent. Timing and spacing are critical for this, as your counter must come out before your opponent can react.

- **Counter-Specific Moves**: Some characters have **counter-specific special moves**, which trigger automatically when they are attacked at the right time. These moves are high-risk but high-reward, often resulting in huge damage or a combo setup.

4.4 Defensive Use of the Rev System

The **Rev System** isn't only a tool for offensive power—it also has defensive applications that can significantly impact the outcome of a match.

Using the Rev System for Defense

When the **Rev Gauge** is filled, players can use it defensively to protect themselves and turn the tide of battle.

- **Rev Move Defensive Benefits**: A **Rev Move** can provide defensive buffs, such as faster recovery from blocks, enhanced evasion techniques, or the ability to perform a counter-attack more effectively.

- **Invincibility Frames**: Some **Rev Moves** provide brief invincibility or reduce the damage taken from attacks, allowing players to escape pressure situations or punish an over-committed opponent.

- **Rev Burst for Countering**: Activating a **Rev Burst** at the right moment can help you break out of an opponent's combo or pressure, allowing you to initiate your own attack immediately.

Strategic Rev Usage

Players must decide when to use their Rev Gauge effectively. Holding on to it for a critical moment or using it as a defensive tool can be the difference between survival and defeat. Using the Rev System defensively requires good foresight, as wasting the gauge on unnecessary actions can leave you vulnerable later in the match.

Chapter 5: Character Roster Overview

5.1 Returning Fighters (Terry, Mai, Joe, Andy, etc.)

The **returning fighters** in *Fatal Fury: City of the Wolves* bring a sense of continuity and nostalgia to the game. These fighters have been iconic staples in the series for years, and their inclusion in the new title maintains their legacy while introducing updates to their move sets, designs, and fighting styles. Let's take a look at some of the key characters who make a return:

Terry Bogard

Terry remains one of the most beloved and recognizable characters in the *Fatal Fury* series. Known for his charismatic personality and powerful moves, Terry's fighting style blends **powerful punches**, **kicks**, and devastating **specials**. His iconic **Power Wave** and **Burn Knuckle** make him a force to be reckoned with.

- **Key Changes**: While Terry's core moveset remains intact, his **new Rev System specials** and **updated combos** give him more options in both offense and defense.

- **Personality**: As always, Terry maintains his "Here's to the next fight!" attitude, a friendly but fierce competitor in the ring.

Mai Shiranui

Mai is a fan-favorite fighter known for her agility, versatility, and seductive persona. As the premier **ninja** in the *Fatal Fury* series, Mai's combination of **quick strikes**, **counters**, and **projectile moves** makes her a well-rounded fighter. Her **Ninja Power** allows her to dart around the screen, controlling space and applying pressure.

- **Key Changes**: Mai's **special moves** are more refined, and she has additional combo chains involving her **Kunoichi Flurry**. Her **Rev System usage** also enhances her defensive capabilities.

- **Personality**: Her playful attitude and flirtatious style remain a core part of her character.

Joe Higashi

Joe's **Muay Thai** fighting style is lethal and precise, characterized by **powerful knees, elbows**, and **throws**. His **speed** and ability to overwhelm opponents with constant pressure have made him a consistent top-tier fighter.

- **Key Changes**: Joe's **new counter-techniques** and **special cancels** are a welcome addition, making him even more dangerous in close-range combat.

- **Personality**: Joe's brashness and bold personality, combined with his confidence, make him a fan favorite.

Andy Bogard

As the younger brother of Terry, Andy brings a more **calculated and strategic approach** to fighting. His **karate** techniques combined with his **quick and precise attacks** make him highly technical and deadly.

- **Key Changes**: Andy's **new mix-ups** with his **Ice Wave** and **Shiranui-ryu** style give him additional options for controlling the fight from mid-range.

- **Personality**: Andy remains a determined and focused fighter, contrasting his brother's brashness.

5.2 New Faces (Vox Reaper, etc.)

Fatal Fury: City of the Wolves introduces several **new characters**, expanding the roster with fresh faces and innovative fighting styles that add more depth and variety to the game. Among these newcomers, **Vox Reaper** stands out as a major addition.

Vox Reaper

Vox Reaper is a **dark, mysterious character** with a unique blend of **swordplay** and **shadow manipulation**. His fighting style revolves around **distance control** and **surprise attacks** from the shadows, making him a highly unpredictable opponent.

- **Fighting Style**: A mix of **ninja techniques** and **swordsmanship**, Vox Reaper uses his weapon to create barriers and unblockable attacks. His **shadow teleportation** allows him to evade attacks and reposition himself at lightning speed.

- **Special Moves**: His **Shadow Slash** and **Reaper's Grasp** can teleport him across the screen, while his **Soul Drain** move absorbs health from opponents temporarily.

- **Personality**: Quiet and menacing, Vox Reaper speaks little but exudes a cold and calculating demeanor. His dark backstory is revealed gradually through his interactions in Story Mode.

Other New Characters

Other new faces include fighters from various backgrounds, each with distinct personalities and combat styles. Characters like **Kaede**

Tsukino, a fierce **karate master** who uses pressure-based fighting tactics, and **Lola Vixen**, a **taekwondo expert** with an emphasis on agility and precision kicks, round out the new roster.

- **Kaede Tsukino**: Her karate style is enhanced by her ability to counter and break through guards. She is an all-around balanced fighter.

- **Lola Vixen**: Using her superior legwork and acrobatic skills, Lola can overwhelm opponents with **quick kicks** and **aerial maneuvers**, providing a unique fast-paced fighting style.

5.3 Guest Fighters (Cristiano Ronaldo, Salvatore Ganacci)

In a surprising twist, *City of the Wolves* introduces **guest fighters** from outside the traditional fighting game world. These characters bring a mix of real-life athleticism and entertainment to the roster.

Cristiano Ronaldo

Cristiano Ronaldo, the football legend, enters the world of *Fatal Fury* as a unique guest fighter. Known for his **agility**, **strength**, and **precision**, Ronaldo uses his football background to deliver powerful **kicks, tackles**, and **goalkeeper-style blocking** techniques.

- **Fighting Style**: Ronaldo incorporates his **football skills** into his moves, with **ball control techniques** and **quick footwork**. He can launch **football projectiles** and use his speed to dodge and counterattack.

- **Special Moves**: Ronaldo's **Ronaldo Kick** can knock opponents across the screen, while his **Free Kick Fury** delivers a powerful shot that can break through defenses.

- **Personality**: Confident and determined, Ronaldo's inclusion adds a fun, charismatic character to the mix, and his rivalry with other guest fighters adds to his competitive nature.

Salvatore Ganacci

Salvatore Ganacci, the music producer and DJ, brings his unique personality and high-energy style to the game. Known for his flashy and unpredictable nature, Ganacci's moves are as eccentric as his appearance.

- **Fighting Style**: Ganacci uses **breakdancing, flamboyant dance moves**, and **electronic beats** to attack and confuse opponents. His moves incorporate rhythms and tempo that disorient foes, making him a tricky fighter to predict.

- **Special Moves**: His **Beat Drop** stuns opponents with a pulse of energy, while his **Electric Spin** involves a rapid spinning kick that hits multiple times.

- **Personality**: Vibrant and eccentric, Salvatore Ganacci adds humor and style to the game, offering a unique character who embodies fun and chaos.

5.4 Character Archetypes & Fighting Styles

Understanding the **archetypes** and **fighting styles** of each character is crucial for effectively mastering the roster. Each character in *City of the Wolves* falls into a specific archetype based on their strengths, weaknesses, and fighting techniques.

Striker Archetype

Strikers focus on **quick, high-damage attacks** and **aggressive playstyles**. These fighters excel at closing the distance and overwhelming their opponents with fast and powerful hits.

- **Examples: Terry Bogard, Joe Higashi, Salvatore Ganacci**.

- **Playstyle**: Focus on **rushdown** strategies, maintaining pressure, and using high-impact moves to break through defenses.

Defender Archetype

Defenders specialize in **counter-attacks**, **guarding**, and **taking control of the match with patience**. They often rely on blocking, evading, and waiting for the right moment to strike back.

- **Examples: Mai Shiranui, Vox Reaper, Cristiano Ronaldo**.

- **Playstyle**: Slow-paced but calculated, focusing on **defensive maneuvers** and waiting for an opening to exploit.

Zoner Archetype

Zoners use **projectiles**, **space control**, and **long-range tactics** to keep their opponents at bay. They rely on their ability to control the pace of the match by dictating the range of combat.

- **Examples**: Andy Bogard, Kaede Tsukino.

- **Playstyle**: Use **long-range specials**, like projectiles or anti-air moves, to control the distance and force the opponent into unfavorable positions.

Hybrid Archetype

Hybrid characters combine elements of both **offensive** and **defensive** strategies. They are flexible and can adapt to any situation, offering a balanced fighting style.

- **Examples**: Lola Vixen, Joe Higashi.

- **Playstyle**: The key is **adaptability**, switching between defensive and offensive tactics as needed, depending on the situation.

Chapter 6: In-Depth Character Guides

6.1 Move Lists & Input Commands

Each character in *Fatal Fury: City of the Wolves* has a unique set of moves that players need to master to fully unlock their potential. This section provides a comprehensive list of each character's **special moves**, **command inputs**, and **normal attacks**. Whether you're looking for basic moves or advanced techniques, this guide will help you execute each character's arsenal efficiently.

Terry Bogard

- **Power Wave** (Quarter Circle Forward + Punch)

- **Burn Knuckle** (Charge Back, Forward + Punch)

- **Rising Tackle** (Charge Down, Up + Punch)

- **Crack Shoot** (Quarter Circle Back + Kick)

- **Buster Wolf** (Quarter Circle Forward x2 + Punch)

- **Super Special Move: Power Geyser** (Quarter Circle Back, Forward + Punch – after full Rev Meter activation)

Mai Shiranui

- **Kunoichi Flurry** (Quarter Circle Forward + Punch)

- **Phoenix Fire** (Quarter Circle Forward + Kick)

- **Shiranui Ninpo** (Charge Down, Up + Punch)

- **Super Special Move: Mai's Shiranui Fury** (Quarter Circle Back x2 + Punch – after full Rev Meter activation)

Joe Higashi

- **Tiger Kick** (Quarter Circle Forward + Kick)

- **Flying Knee** (Charge Down, Up + Kick)

- **Muay Thai Rage** (Quarter Circle Back + Punch)

- **Super Special Move: Hurricane Strike** (Quarter Circle Forward x2 + Kick – after full Rev Meter activation)

Vox Reaper

- **Shadow Slash** (Charge Back, Forward + Punch)

- **Soul Drain** (Charge Down, Up + Kick)

- **Reaper's Grasp** (Quarter Circle Forward + Punch)

- **Super Special Move: Eclipse of the Soul** (Quarter Circle Back x2 + Punch – after full Rev Meter activation)

Cristiano Ronaldo

- **Ronaldo Kick** (Quarter Circle Forward + Kick)

- **Free Kick Fury** (Charge Back, Forward + Punch)

- **Footwork Master** (Quarter Circle Down + Punch)

- **Super Special Move: Goalkeeper's Rage** (Quarter Circle Forward x2 + Kick – after full Rev Meter activation)

6.2 Strategy & Best Matchups

In *Fatal Fury: City of the Wolves*, understanding your character's strengths and weaknesses is key to winning. Each fighter excels in certain matchups based on their **fighting style** and **move set**. This section will provide strategies for maximizing your character's effectiveness and guide you through the **best matchups** against other characters.

Terry Bogard

- **Strategy**: Terry excels in **rushdown** and **mix-ups**, using his speed to close the distance. His powerful **Burn Knuckle** and **Power Wave** allow him to control the pace, while **Rising Tackle** serves as an excellent anti-air option.

- **Best Matchups**:

- **Joe Higashi**: Terry's mix-ups and aerial control make him highly effective against Joe's more linear Muay Thai approach.

- **Vox Reaper**: Terry's speed and pressure make him a good counter to Vox's shadow manipulation.

Mai Shiranui

- **Strategy**: Mai is a **technical fighter** who excels at baiting opponents with her **quick dash attacks** and **nimble movement**. Her **Phoenix Fire** and **Kunoichi Flurry** are great tools to control space and apply pressure.

- **Best Matchups**:

  - **Andy Bogard**: Mai's speed and her ability to counter Andy's long-range attacks with **Phoenix Fire** and **Shiranui Ninpo** give her an advantage.

  - **Cristiano Ronaldo**: Mai's agility and movement can evade Ronaldo's slower, but powerful kicks.

Joe Higashi

- **Strategy**: Joe's **Muay Thai** fighting style excels in **close-range combat**, using quick strikes, elbows, and knees. Joe excels in applying constant pressure with his **Flying Knee** and **Tiger Kick**.

- **Best Matchups**:

- **Vox Reaper**: Joe's ability to apply pressure can overwhelm Vox's attempts to control space with his shadow-based attacks.

- **Lola Vixen**: Joe's mix-ups and solid defense make him a strong counter to fast, agile characters like Lola, as his attacks can interrupt her aerial assault.

Vox Reaper

- **Strategy**: Vox is a **zoning** and **counter-based** fighter, using his teleportation and shadow powers to control the flow of the match. He excels at confusing opponents and punishing overly aggressive play.

- **Best Matchups**:

  - **Terry Bogard**: Vox's shadow moves give him the ability to dodge Terry's fast attacks and punish him when he overcommits.

  - **Mai Shiranui**: Vox's teleportation and shadow attacks can catch Mai off guard, especially if she relies too heavily on her close-range attacks.

6.3 Combos & Rev Techniques

Executing **combos** and utilizing the **Rev System** effectively are key components in maximizing a character's potential. Each character has unique combo strings, and understanding how to perform these, especially with the added **Rev techniques**, can make a huge difference in competitive play.

Terry Bogard

- **Basic Combos**:

  - Light Punch → Light Kick → Power Wave

  - Burn Knuckle → Crack Shoot → Power Geyser

- **Rev Technique**:

  - **Rev Burst Combo**: Using a **Rev Burst** during a Power Wave creates a **multi-hit combo**, knocking the opponent into the air for a follow-up **Burn Knuckle** for extra damage.

Mai Shiranui

- **Basic Combos**:

  - Light Punch → Phoenix Fire → Kunoichi Flurry

  - Shiranui Ninpo → Light Kick → Phoenix Fire

- **Rev Technique**:

  - **Shiranui Fury Rev Combo**: Using a full **Rev Meter**, Mai can unleash a **Shiranui Fury** combo that deals high damage and leaves the opponent in a stunned state, allowing for another combo chain.

Joe Higashi

- **Basic Combos**:

    - Light Punch → Flying Knee → Tiger Kick

    - Muay Thai Rage → Flying Knee → Hurricane Strike

- **Rev Technique**:

    - **Hurricane Rev Combo**: Using a **Rev Burst** activates **Hurricane Strike**, sending the opponent to the corner, followed by a quick **Flying Knee** for maximum corner pressure.

Vox Reaper

- **Basic Combos**:

    - Shadow Slash → Soul Drain → Reaper's Grasp

    - Light Punch → Shadow Slash → Soul Drain

- **Rev Technique**:

    - **Eclipse of the Soul Rev Combo**: Vox Reaper's ultimate technique, **Eclipse of the Soul**, can be followed up by an extended combo of **Shadow Slash** and **Reaper's Grasp**, ensuring the opponent takes full damage from the **Eclipse**.

6.4 Style Customization & Loadouts

In *Fatal Fury: City of the Wolves*, **style customization** and **loadouts** allow players to tailor their characters to fit their preferred playstyle. Whether you want to focus on **offensive power**, **defensive resilience**, or **agility**, the game gives you the tools to modify each character's attributes.

Terry Bogard

- **Custom Style 1**:

  - **Focus**: Speed and Aggression

  - **Key Attributes**: Increased movement speed and **lower cooldown on special moves**.

  - **Recommended Loadout**: **Offensive Gear** (Boosts Power Wave and Buster Wolf range).

- **Custom Style 2**:

  - **Focus**: Defensive Play and Counters

  - **Key Attributes**: Enhanced defense and **faster Rev Charge**.

  - **Recommended Loadout**: **Counter Gear** (Increases power of counter-attacks after perfect guard).

Mai Shiranui

- **Custom Style 1**:

    - **Focus**: Agility and Mobility

    - **Key Attributes**: Increased movement speed and **faster recovery** after moves.

    - **Recommended Loadout**: **Mobility Gear** (Increases the speed of aerial attacks and evasions).

- **Custom Style 2**:

    - **Focus**: Pressure and Control

    - **Key Attributes**: Enhanced **combo length** and **multi-hit attack range**.

    - **Recommended Loadout**: **Pressure Gear** (Boosts Kunoichi Flurry and Phoenix Fire).

Joe Higashi

- **Custom Style 1**:

    - **Focus**: All-around Fighter

    - **Key Attributes**: Balanced **strength and defense**, perfect for both offense and defense.

- o **Recommended Loadout**: **Balanced Gear** (Enhances both Muay Thai Rage and Tiger Kick).

- **Custom Style 2**:

  - o **Focus**: Aggressive Pressure

  - o **Key Attributes**: Increased **damage output** and **faster special moves**.

  - o **Recommended Loadout**: **Aggression Gear** (Increases the damage of Flying Knee and Hurricane Strike).

Chapter 7: Stages, Arenas & Environmental Factors

7.1 Stage List & Descriptions

Fatal Fury: City of the Wolves features a wide variety of **stages** that offer unique environments, setting the tone for each battle. From bustling cities to serene mountaintops, these stages provide a rich backdrop for intense combat. Here's a list of key stages in the game, along with a brief description of each:

1. South Town Streets

- **Description**: The iconic **South Town**, known for being the home turf of many *Fatal Fury* characters, makes a return. The **downtown area** is packed with neon lights, a bustling crowd, and a dynamic urban atmosphere. **Cars** and **pedestrians** occasionally move in the background, adding life to the stage.

- **Environment**: Concrete jungle with a neon-lit skyline. Urban sounds fill the air, with occasional honks and people chatting.

2. Mai's Dojo

- **Description**: Set in a peaceful **traditional dojo** surrounded by serene gardens, this stage represents **Mai Shiranui's** roots. The **wooden flooring** and **bamboo fences** create a tranquil yet intense atmosphere. A **hot spring** sits in the background, with koi fish swimming.

- **Environment**: A calm, spiritual vibe contrasted by fierce fighting. Birds chirp, and the sound of flowing water can be heard.

3. Mount Fuji Cliffs

- **Description**: A picturesque stage perched on the edge of **Mount Fuji**, overlooking expansive views of the Japanese landscape. **Cherry blossoms** fall gently from trees, adding beauty to the danger of the cliffside battle. One wrong move, and you'll be sent tumbling down the mountain.

- **Environment**: A blend of calm natural beauty and the looming danger of the cliffside. A wind gently blows through, and the distant sound of waterfalls can be heard.

4. The Underground Arena

- **Description**: Located beneath the streets of South Town, this **dark, gritty underground fighting pit** is filled with flashing lights and booming music. The audience's cheers echo off the walls as combatants face off in an environment designed for brutality and spectacle.

- **Environment**: Neon lights, chain-link fences, and exposed steel beams set the stage for brutal brawls. The echoing sounds of cheers and the beat of electronic music create an intense atmosphere.

5. Desert Oasis

- **Description**: A unique setting where fighters clash in an **arid desert landscape**, complete with a **small oasis** surrounded by towering dunes. The sun blazes overhead, casting long shadows as combatants fight beneath the intense heat. Occasionally, **sandstorms** can appear in the background, adding dynamic elements.

- **Environment**: The sound of shifting sand and occasional gusts of wind. The atmosphere is hot and oppressive, with shifting shadows cast by the dunes.

6. Raging Storm Peak

- **Description**: A **mountainous stage** where nature itself seems to be in a constant state of chaos. **Thunderstorms** rage in the background, with the occasional **lightning strike** lighting up the sky. Strong winds whip through the stage, affecting movement and strategy.

- **Environment**: Storm clouds loom overhead, and the howling winds create an intimidating environment. Lightning flashes intermittently, casting brief, dramatic light over the battleground.

7. Tokyo Night Skyline

- **Description**: A vibrant city stage set on a rooftop in the heart of **Tokyo**. The skyline sparkles in the background, and **helicopters** fly overhead. The fighting area is surrounded by **neon signs**, creating a stark contrast between beauty and the brutality of the battle.

- **Environment**: The sounds of traffic and distant city noises fill the air. The cold wind of the night and occasional flashing lights set the tone for high-flying action.

7.2 Interactive Elements & Hazards

Some stages in *Fatal Fury: City of the Wolves* contain **interactive elements** and **hazards** that can dramatically affect the outcome of a battle. These elements create opportunities for **creative strategies** or challenge players to adjust their tactics on the fly.

1. South Town Streets: Traffic Hazards

- **Interactive Element**: Occasionally, **cars** drive across the stage, creating a **moving hazard** that can knock players off balance. If an opponent is caught by a car, they take **damage** and are briefly stunned.

- **Strategy Tip**: Use the traffic as a shield or to confuse your opponent, but avoid getting caught in its path.

2. Mai's Dojo: Koi Pond

- **Interactive Element**: **Koi fish** swim through a **small pond** near the edge of the stage. If an opponent is knocked into the pond, they take **small damage** over time as they struggle to get out.

- **Strategy Tip**: You can push an opponent towards the koi pond to take advantage of the environmental hazard.

However, be cautious of falling in yourself.

3. Mount Fuji Cliffs: Cliffside Drops

- **Hazard**: The edge of the stage is precarious. If a fighter is knocked too close to the edge, they risk falling off the cliff and **losing the round**.

- **Interactive Element**: A **wind gust** occasionally sweeps across the stage, affecting movement and jumping. Players must time their attacks carefully to avoid being blown off balance.

4. Underground Arena: Ring Obstacles

- **Interactive Element**: The **chain-link fencing** around the arena can be used for **wall jumps** or as a **springboard** for attacks. However, the fencing can be broken if an opponent lands a heavy attack, creating an opening in the defense.

- **Hazard**: **Falling debris** occasionally hits the ring, damaging both players for a short time.

5. Desert Oasis: Sandstorms

- **Hazard**: Every so often, a **sandstorm** rolls through, reducing visibility and making attacks harder to predict. Players must adjust their timing and distance during these storms.

- **Interactive Element**: The **oasis** offers the chance to recover health when standing in its cool waters, but only briefly, as stepping out causes a quick return to the scorching heat.

6. Raging Storm Peak: Lightning Strikes

- **Hazard**: **Lightning strikes** from the storm occasionally hit the stage. Fighters standing in the strike zone will take **massive electrical damage**.

- **Interactive Element**: The storm's powerful winds can **alter jump arcs** and affect projectile trajectories, making long-range attacks more unpredictable.

7. Tokyo Night Skyline: Helicopter Attacks

- **Interactive Element**: A **helicopter** occasionally flies by, dropping **flashbangs** or small explosive devices onto the rooftop. Fighters caught in the blast take **damage** and are stunned briefly.

- **Hazard**: The **rooftop** is small, leaving little room to maneuver, making it easier for players to fall off the edge after a strong attack.

7.3 Dynamic Stage Transitions

Some stages feature **dynamic transitions** that affect the flow of battle, either by changing the environment or introducing new hazards mid-fight. These transitions add an extra layer of strategy, as players need to adapt quickly to shifting conditions.

1. South Town Streets to Alleyway

- **Transition**: After a certain time, the fight may shift from the **main street** to a narrow **alleyway**. The transition creates a **more confined environment**, forcing players to adjust to **tighter combat**.

- **Strategy Tip**: Use the alleyway to your advantage by using **corner pressure** or crowding your opponent against the walls for combos.

2. Mai's Dojo to Secret Shrine

- **Transition**: Mid-match, the battle may transition into the **hidden shrine** behind Mai's dojo. The environment becomes more **mystical**, with **floating lanterns** and **tighter platforms**.

- **Strategy Tip**: The shrine setting can benefit agile fighters, offering a lot of space for aerial combat and dodging.

3. Mount Fuji Cliffs to Ice Cavern

- **Transition**: A **frosty cavern** appears after a powerful attack or time elapsed, changing the scenery dramatically. Ice **makes the ground slippery**, affecting movement and jump height.

- **Strategy Tip**: Use the ice to create unpredictable movements, but be careful not to slip or misjudge your positioning.

4. Underground Arena to Rooftop Battle

- **Transition**: After a set time, the fight shifts from the **underground pit** to the **rooftop**, offering a more open environment but with risks of falling off the edge.

- **Strategy Tip**: The verticality of the rooftop offers opportunities for high-risk, high-reward aerial attacks.

7.4 Stage Selection Strategy

Choosing the right stage is crucial to gaining the upper hand in battle. The stage selection can dramatically affect your fighting style and tactics.

1. Close-Quarters Combat

If you prefer **close-range combat** and overwhelming your opponent with pressure, choose stages with **confined spaces** like the **Underground Arena** or **Tokyo Night Skyline**. These stages limit the ability to retreat or reposition, forcing both players to engage in intense fights.

2. Agility & Mobility

For more **agile** characters or those relying on quick dodges, jumping, and aerial attacks, stages like **Mai's Dojo** or **Mount Fuji Cliffs** provide open spaces and room to move freely. Use these stages to take advantage of your character's speed and dexterity.

3. Environmental Hazards

If your playstyle focuses on **outsmarting** or **setting traps** for your opponent, select stages like **Raging Storm Peak** or **Desert Oasis**, where **dynamic hazards** and **environmental factors** can be used to your advantage.

4. Zoning & Long-Range Play

If you're playing a **zoner** who relies on keeping distance, the **South Town Streets** or **Tokyo Night Skyline** offer large spaces to maintain pressure and control the pace of the fight. Make use of the environment to restrict your opponent's movement while maintaining your long-range advantages.

Chapter 8: Multiplayer & Online Strategy

8.1 Ranked vs Casual Play

In *Fatal Fury: City of the Wolves*, **multiplayer** is an essential component of the game. The game offers two primary types of online play: **Ranked** and **Casual**. Both modes offer different experiences and cater to different playstyles. Understanding the differences between them will help you maximize your competitive edge.

Ranked Play

- **Purpose**: Ranked matches are designed for **competitive players** looking to climb the leaderboards and prove their skills against others. The system uses a **rating or ranking system** that adjusts based on your performance, so the more wins you rack up, the higher your rank.

- **Matchmaking**: In Ranked, you'll face opponents at a similar skill level, and the match is taken seriously with the intent to win. Each match has significant **consequences** for both your ranking and **confidence**.

- **Strategy Tip**: Focus on **refining** your character knowledge, **matchup strategies**, and **mental resilience**. Ranked play rewards consistency, so avoid taking unnecessary risks or trying out new tactics mid-match.

Casual Play

- **Purpose**: Casual matches are for **relaxed, fun** gameplay where the stakes are lower. You can try new characters, strategies, and combos without worrying about the effects on your ranking.

- **Matchmaking**: Casual mode offers looser matchmaking, so you might find yourself facing opponents of varying skill levels. It's more about **experimentation** and **learning** rather than competing for rank.

- **Strategy Tip**: Use Casual play to **experiment** with different characters and strategies. This mode is perfect for practicing specific moves, combos, and character mechanics.

8.2 Building a Competitive Loadout

In *Fatal Fury: City of the Wolves*, **loadouts** are an essential aspect of preparing for online play. A **competitive loadout** refers to the gear, styles, and tactics you bring into battle. Building a strong loadout can make a huge difference in both **Ranked** and **Casual** matches.

1. Character Choice

- **Choosing the Right Character**: First and foremost, your character choice should align with your personal playstyle. If you're a **rushdown** player, characters like **Terry Bogard** or **Joe Higashi** may suit you. For a more **zoning-oriented** approach, try characters like **Vox Reaper** or **Cristiano Ronaldo**.

- **Character Familiarity**: It's essential to **master one or two characters** thoroughly rather than trying to be good at all. **Practice makes perfect**, and knowing your character's move list, combos, and strategies inside-out will give you an edge over less prepared opponents.

2. Style Customization

- **Offensive or Defensive Loadout**: Decide whether you want to focus on **aggressive rushdown** or **defensive counterplay**. Aggressive loadouts will prioritize **damage**, **speed**, and **combo execution**, while defensive loadouts will focus on **stamina**, **counterattacks**, and **escaping pressure**.

- **Recommended Gear**:

    - For **offensive play**, use **Aggression Gear** to boost attack speed and combo extension.

    - For **defensive play**, consider **Defensive Gear** to enhance **block strength**, **rev burst recovery**, and **counter ability**.

3. Experimenting with Loadouts

- **Balancing Stats**: Balancing your loadout is key. For example, **offensive-focused** gear may make your character fast but weak in defense. If you find that you're getting overwhelmed, consider adjusting your loadout to balance **defense** and **mobility**.

- **Special Loadout for Ranked**: In Ranked play, focus on a loadout that provides **reliable damage** output and **resilience**. Be careful of focusing too much on novelty or style at the cost of practicality. A well-rounded loadout is often more consistent in competitive play.

8.3 Lag & Netcode Optimization Tips

Playing online means dealing with **internet connectivity** and **lag**, which can make or break your gameplay experience. Understanding how **lag** affects your matches and optimizing your connection can give you a huge advantage in online battles.

1. Understanding Lag and Input Delay

- **Lag**: Lag is a delay between the inputs you make on your controller and what is shown on screen. It can cause **input delays** or even make the game seem unresponsive. Lag is most noticeable when you're trying to **execute combos** or **block** at crucial moments.

- **Netcode**: The netcode used by the game determines how well the game compensates for lag. Good netcode smooths over delays and reduces the amount of stutter or inconsistency you experience in the match.

2. Optimizing Your Internet Connection

- **Wired vs. Wireless**: Always use a **wired connection** if possible. **Ethernet cables** provide a more stable and reliable connection than wireless internet, reducing the chances of **connection drops** or lag spikes.

- **Closing Background Applications**: If you're using a PC or console, ensure **no background applications** (such as streaming or downloading) are using up bandwidth while playing. These can cause significant delays in your online experience.

- **Optimal Connection**: If you can, choose **servers** with the **lowest ping**. This reduces the distance your data travels and can minimize lag.

3. Adjusting Game Settings for Better Performance

- **Graphics Settings**: Lowering certain graphics settings, such as **motion blur** or **shadow quality**, can help reduce the load on your system and improve overall game performance, especially in **higher-traffic** areas of the stage.

- **Input Delay Settings**: Some games offer an **input delay slider** or **frame buffer options** to tweak the balance between graphics and performance. Experiment with these settings to find the sweet spot.

4. Choosing the Right Matchmaking Region

- Always try to connect with players in regions closer to you. This minimizes lag and results in a smoother experience. Most matchmaking systems will automatically choose the **best region**, but if you're having consistent issues, manually adjusting your region might help.

8.4 Reading Your Opponent

One of the key components to **winning multiplayer matches** is the ability to **read your opponent**. This skill is crucial in both **Ranked** and **Casual play**, as understanding how your opponent plays can give you the upper hand.

1. Observe the Playstyle

- **Aggression vs. Patience**: Some players are highly **aggressive**, constantly rushing in and looking for opportunities to land quick hits or combos. Others may be more **defensive**, waiting for the perfect moment to counterattack. Identifying this early can help you adjust your approach accordingly.

  - If your opponent is aggressive, **block** and punish with fast counters or **long-range projectiles**.

  - If your opponent is defensive, look for opportunities to create **pressure** and force mistakes.

2. Identifying Weaknesses

- **Overuse of Attacks**: Many players will rely on a few **signature moves**. If you notice an opponent spamming a move, try to **counter it** or bait them into a mistake.

- **Patterns**: Watch for any **repetitive behaviors**. For example, if your opponent consistently jumps after blocking, you can counter with an anti-air move. If they always rush in after performing a combo, consider using a **throw** or

counter move.

3. Adapting During the Match

- **Changing Tactics**: If you feel your opponent is adjusting to your strategy, you should also be ready to change up your own tactics. If they've started reading your combos or defense, switch things up with different **approaches** or **mind games**.

- **Baiting and Punishing**: In higher-level play, you can try to **bait** an opponent into attacking early by showing openings or vulnerable moments. Once they commit, **punish** their decision.

4. Mental Game & Mindset

- Stay calm under pressure. **Reading your opponent** isn't just about understanding their moves but also about maintaining **mental clarity**. Take note of their tendencies but don't become predictable yourself.

- Sometimes the most important element of reading your opponent is **reading their psychology**—predicting what they will do next based on their behavior and personality.

Chapter 9: Unlockables, Easter Eggs & Secrets

9.1 Hidden Characters & Costumes

In *Fatal Fury: City of the Wolves*, there are a variety of **hidden characters** and **alternate costumes** that can be unlocked through specific actions or conditions. These additions add significant replay value and a sense of discovery for players who enjoy completing every facet of the game.

1. Hidden Characters

- **Vox Reaper (Unlockable)**: One of the most anticipated characters, **Vox Reaper**, can be unlocked by completing the game on **Hard Mode** without continuing. After this, a special in-game **event** unlocks Vox, revealing his backstory and unique abilities.

- **Cristiano Ronaldo (Guest Fighter)**: This **guest character** can be unlocked by completing a specific set of challenges in **Arcade Mode**. This involves defeating certain characters within a time limit and without losing a match.

- **Salvatore Ganacci (Guest Fighter)**: Another guest fighter who becomes available once players unlock all of the game's **main stages**. Completing a series of **hidden objectives** on each stage will allow you to face Ganacci and unlock him as a playable character.

- **Unlock Method**: To access hidden characters, pay close attention to **special requirements**, including completing certain modes under specific conditions, achieving high scores, or facing secret **bosses**.

2. Unlockable Costumes

- **Classic Skins**: Many characters, such as **Terry Bogard** and **Mai Shiranui**, have **classic skins** (based on their appearances in earlier *Fatal Fury* or *King of Fighters* games). These can be unlocked through **Arcade Mode** or by completing **specific challenges** related to each character.

- **Alternate Outfits**: Some characters have **alternate costumes** tied to their personality or story arcs. For example, **Joe Higashi's** alternate outfit is unlocked after defeating him in **Story Mode** with a **specific character**.

- **Special Theme Costumes**: In celebration of specific in-game events or milestones, you can unlock **seasonal outfits** or **themed costumes** for certain characters, such as **summer beach outfits** or **winter festival gear**. These are usually available after achieving **100% completion** in **Arcade Mode**.

9.2 Unlockable Stages & Themes

In addition to characters and costumes, *Fatal Fury: City of the Wolves* features **hidden stages** and **unlockable themes** that add a layer of variety to the game's environments and settings.

1. Hidden Stages

- **Vox's Hideout**: To unlock this **secret stage**, you need to **defeat Vox Reaper** in **Arcade Mode** under **specific conditions** (e.g., without losing a round). The stage is set in a **dark, mysterious** underground lair, full of **dark lighting, pulsing energy**, and **ominous music**.

- **Ganacci's Club**: This **exclusive stage** can be unlocked by defeating **Salvatore Ganacci** after completing a set of **timed challenges**. It features a **club setting** with vibrant neon lights and a pulsating electronic soundtrack, adding a different vibe to the game's more traditional fighting arenas.

- **Tokyo Rooftop Party**: This special **nighttime rooftop stage** is unlocked after completing **Story Mode** with a **perfect win** (no damage taken). It features stunning views of **Tokyo, fireworks**, and a festive party atmosphere, making it perfect for high-energy battles.

2. Unlockable Themes

- **Dynamic Music Themes**: Each hidden stage comes with **unique music** that matches the tone of the environment. For example, **Vox's Hideout** has an eerie, **ambient** track, while **Ganacci's Club** boasts **electronic beats** that sync with the neon vibe of the stage.

- **Environmental Variations**: Some stages have **day/night cycles**, changing their atmosphere based on the time of day. This can affect the visibility and even the types of environmental hazards or interactive elements in the stage.

9.3 Easter Eggs & Series References

Fatal Fury: City of the Wolves is packed with **Easter eggs** and **references** to the *Fatal Fury* and *King of Fighters* series. Fans of the franchise will enjoy the numerous nods to the past, hidden features, and secret interactions throughout the game.

1. Classic Cameos

- **Geese Howard's Portrait**: In certain stages, you'll notice **Geese Howard's portrait** hanging on the wall, a nod to his iconic role in the *Fatal Fury* series. There's also a hidden **soundbite** when interacting with these portraits that quotes his famous lines from previous games.

- **Iori Yagami's Teaser**: In one of the **hidden stages**, you'll find a **graffiti mural** of **Iori Yagami**, a popular character from *King of Fighters*. This is a subtle teaser that may indicate a future crossover or character appearance.

- **Classic Soundtrack Remixes**: During specific moments in **Arcade Mode**, you might hear **remixed versions** of classic *Fatal Fury* and *King of Fighters* tracks. These are Easter eggs designed for long-time fans of the series.

2. Secret Dialogues

- Some **hidden dialogues** occur between characters during specific moments in **Story Mode**. These include references to past games, iconic moments, and even **insider jokes** aimed at loyal fans. For instance, a conversation between **Mai Shiranui** and **Andy Bogard** might include a cheeky reference to the events of earlier titles.

- **Character Rivalries**: As part of the Easter eggs, certain **rival characters** (like **Terry** and **Geese**) might exchange unique **rivalry lines** when they face each other in battle. These lines are often callbacks to pivotal story moments in previous *Fatal Fury* and *King of Fighters* games.

3. Unlockable Sound Effects

- **Retro Sound Effects**: By completing **certain tasks** or achieving **specific milestones**, players can unlock **retro sound effects** from the earlier games in the franchise. For example, the **classic KO sound** or **win quotes** from older titles can be activated during fights.

- **Secret Interactions**: Some stages feature **hidden interactions** if you use specific attacks or interact with objects in the environment. For example, using a **throw move** in **Mai's Dojo** might trigger a short **cutscene** where **Mai's father** watches from the background.

9.4 Tips for 100% Completion

Achieving **100% completion** in *Fatal Fury: City of the Wolves* requires a mix of skill, perseverance, and exploration. Here's how you can maximize your progress and unlock all of the game's secrets:

1. Completing the Story Mode

- **Story Paths**: Play through **Story Mode** multiple times to unlock different **branching paths** and alternate storylines. This will help you uncover all the hidden characters, dialogue, and stages tied to these paths.

- **Challenge Mode**: To unlock certain hidden characters, you'll need to complete **Challenge Mode** where you face **unique objectives** (e.g., win without taking damage, use specific techniques, etc.).

- **Achieving Perfect Wins**: Aim to complete **Story Mode** and **Arcade Mode** with **perfect wins** (no damage). This often unlocks rare costumes and stages.

2. Mastering Arcade Mode

- **Play on Hard Difficulty**: Completing **Arcade Mode** on **Hard difficulty** without using continues will unlock many of the game's more difficult-to-access secrets, including hidden characters and special cutscenes.

- **Secret Boss Fights**: During your Arcade runs, certain conditions will trigger secret boss fights against **powerful characters**. Defeating these bosses unlocks exclusive rewards, including **alternate endings**.

3. Collecting All Achievements

- **Achievements**: Keep an eye on the in-game **achievement list**. Many unlockables are tied to specific achievements, such as **win a match in every stage, perform every combo move**, or **defeat every hidden boss**.

- **Special Tasks**: Some unlockables can only be accessed after completing **multiple tasks**, such as unlocking all **hidden characters** or completing the game with every character.

4. Secret Trophies

- Hidden **trophies** and **achievements** are scattered throughout the game. For example, there might be a **secret trophy** for defeating the final boss **without using a single Super Move**, or for performing a **perfect combo** that stretches through the entire round.

- **Track Progress**: Keep a checklist of what you've unlocked and what remains. Use the **Challenge Mode** to track progress on each task and focus on the ones that provide the most significant rewards.

Chapter 10: Advanced Techniques & Meta Play

10.1 Frame Data & Hitbox Mastery

Mastering **frame data** and **hitboxes** is essential for any player looking to elevate their game and compete at a high level. Understanding how moves interact with each other in terms of speed, range, and recovery time is a critical skill in *Fatal Fury: City of the Wolves*.

1. Frame Data Basics

- **What is Frame Data?** Frame data refers to the number of **frames** it takes for a move to **execute**, **hit**, and **recover**. In fighting games, every action (attack, block, dodge, etc.) happens within **frames**. For instance, a move that takes **3 frames** to execute is faster than a move that takes **5 frames**.

- **Startup, Active, and Recovery Frames**:

    - **Startup**: The number of frames before a move becomes active.

    - **Active**: The frames where the move can hit or affect the opponent.

    - **Recovery**: The frames after the move where the character is vulnerable and cannot act again.

2. Understanding Hitboxes

- **What are Hitboxes?** A **hitbox** is an invisible area that determines whether an attack connects with the opponent. Knowing the **size** and **location** of a move's hitbox can help you determine if an attack will land or be blocked.

- **Character-Specific Hitboxes**: Every character in *Fatal Fury: City of the Wolves* has unique hitboxes for their **normal attacks**, **special moves**, and **super moves**. Learning each character's hitbox interactions is crucial for **spacing** and **combos**.

- **Hitbox Visuals**: Some training modes may allow you to view **hitbox overlays** to help you better understand the exact range and timing of your moves.

3. Frame Data in Practice

- **Punishing Unsafe Moves**: Knowing frame data helps you identify **unsafe moves** that leave an opponent open for a **punish**. For example, if you know your opponent's attack has a **long recovery time** and you have a fast move, you can **interrupt** their attack and gain the advantage.

- **Safe on Block**: Frame data can also tell you if an attack is **safe on block** (meaning the opponent cannot easily punish it). Moves that are **safe** allow for continuous pressure, while **unsafe** moves can be punished if blocked.

10.2 Mix-ups, Pressure, and Punishes

Creating **unpredictability** through **mix-ups** and applying **constant pressure** are essential to controlling the pace of the match. Mastering these techniques allows you to break through your opponent's defense and secure victories.

1. Mix-up Techniques

- **What is a Mix-up?** A **mix-up** refers to a set of tactics used to confuse or force mistakes from your opponent. This includes using a mix of **high/low attacks**, **throws**, and **overhead** moves to keep the opponent guessing.

- **High/Low Mix-ups**: Use **low attacks** (like crouching kicks or sweeps) to force the opponent into blocking low, and then use **overhead attacks** (like jumping or standing heavy attacks) to catch them off guard.

- **Throw Mix-ups**: Throwing becomes a critical component when your opponent gets **too comfortable** with blocking or reacting. Mix in **throws** to counter players who are overly defensive.

2. Pressure Techniques

- **Constant Pressure**: Keep the pressure on your opponent by chaining attacks together and **keeping them on the defensive**. This can force them to make mistakes and leave openings for larger combos.

- **Frame Traps**: Use attacks that leave your opponent with limited options, forcing them into situations where they either have to block or get hit by your next move.

- **Close-Range Pressure**: In close-range combat, you can use fast **light attacks** to quickly break through an opponent's guard or set up for a **throw**. Apply pressure consistently without overextending, as this could leave you open to a counterattack.

3. Punishing Unsafe Moves

- **Recognizing Unsafe Attacks**: If your opponent uses a **high-risk, high-reward move**, it often comes with a **long recovery time**. Punish these moves by waiting for the recovery window and then counterattacking with your fastest option.

- **Combo Punishes**: If you land a successful counter-hit, follow up with a **combo** to maximize your damage output. Knowing which moves to punish and when to punish them can dramatically improve your efficiency in matches.

- **Teching Throws**: Learn to **tech throws**—breaking free from your opponent's throw attempts. This is crucial for maintaining offensive pressure and avoiding unnecessary damage.

10.3 Tournament Play Essentials

When it comes to competitive play, especially in **tournament settings**, you need to fine-tune your **mental game** and **advanced strategies** to stay ahead of your competition.

1. Preparation for Tournaments

- **Character Mastery**: In a tournament, the most successful players tend to be those who have **mastered a few characters** deeply rather than those who spread themselves thin with many characters. **Choose your main** character and understand their strengths, weaknesses, and matchups.

- **Research Opponents**: In online tournaments or local tournaments, it's crucial to **study your opponents** if possible. Watch their match videos, learn their tendencies, and develop a strategy to counter their playstyle.

- **Practice Mental Focus**: Tournaments can bring in high-pressure situations. Ensure you're mentally prepared for long, intense matches. A calm mind allows for **better decision-making**, **reaction times**, and **adaptation**.

2. Match Mentality

- **First-to-3/First-to-5**: Most tournaments will have **best-of-three** or **best-of-five** formats. It's important to pace yourself and **remain adaptable** during these matches. Losing the first round doesn't mean defeat—adaptation is key.

- **Staying Calm Under Pressure**: In high-stakes tournaments, it's essential to keep your cool even when the match isn't going your way. **Mistakes** and **setbacks** are part of the game, and staying calm will allow you to **reset** and strategize for the next round.

3. Tournament Etiquette

- **Respect Your Opponents**: Always be respectful to fellow players, whether you win or lose. **Sportsmanship** is essential in tournaments, and respectful conduct enhances the experience for everyone involved.

- **Managing Time and Breaks**: **Proper hydration, rest**, and **breaks** between matches are important for maintaining peak performance. Don't skip your mental breaks, even between rounds.

10.4 Post-Launch Updates & DLC Strategy

In the world of modern fighting games, **post-launch updates** and **DLC** content can significantly impact the **meta** and how players approach the game. Staying up-to-date with these changes can help you maintain an edge over other players.

1. Post-Launch Patches

- **Balancing Adjustments**: *Fatal Fury: City of the Wolves* is likely to receive **balance updates** after launch, adjusting character strengths and weaknesses based on community feedback and tournament results. Keep an eye on **patch notes** to stay informed on any changes to **frame data**, **move sets**, or character stats.

- **Meta Shifts**: Sometimes, a **single update** can drastically alter the **meta** by making certain characters or strategies more viable. Being adaptable and learning how the latest patch affects your character is key to staying competitive.

2. DLC Fighters

- **New Character Releases**: As DLC fighters are released, they often come with new strategies and unique playstyles that can shake up the competitive scene. **Experiment with new characters** as they're released and incorporate them into your tournament preparation.

- **Fighter Trends**: The introduction of **new fighters** can often lead to trends in character selection. For example, a **new DLC character** may introduce a powerful **counterplay mechanic** that forces players to adapt their strategies and team compositions.

3. DLC Stages & Features

- **New Stages**: Post-launch DLC may also include **new stages** with unique features that change how characters perform. Some DLC stages might have **interactive elements** or **hazards**, requiring players to **adjust their strategies** when selecting stages in tournaments.

- **New Features**: Keep an eye on additional **features** added in DLCs, such as new **training tools**, **costumes**, or **gameplay modes** that could offer new **meta-breaking strategies** or **opportunities for improvement**.

4. Strategic Planning for DLC

- **Maximizing DLC Value**: If you're serious about the competitive scene, make sure to stay up to date with **DLC releases** and **strategic adjustments** that may come with them. This includes analyzing how **new characters** interact with your current lineup and understanding **new strategies** brought by **updated mechanics**.

- **Community Impact**: Be mindful of how the community reacts to new content. If a new fighter or stage has a **significant impact** on the **meta**, be sure to **adapt** and learn the ins and outs of the new additions before your next tournament.

www.ingramcontent.com/pod-product-compliance
Lightning Source LLC
LaVergne TN
LVHW051715050326
832903LV00032B/4219